DELICIOUS
DIPS

DELICIOUS DIPS

MORE THAN 50 RECIPES FOR DIPS FROM FRESH AND TANGY TO RICH AND CREAMY

RYLAND PETERS & SMALL
LONDON • NEW YORK

Designers Paul Stradling and Emily Breen
Production Mai-Ling Collyer
Art Director Leslie Harrington
Editorial Director Julia Charles
Publisher Cindy Richards

Indexer Hilary Bird

First published in 2017. This revised
edition published in 2020 by
Ryland Peters & Small
20–21 Jockey's Fields
London
WC1R 4BW
and
341 E 116th St
New York
NY 10029

www.rylandpeters.com

Recipe collection compiled by Julia Charles.
Text © Ghillie Başan, Jordan Bourke, Chloe
Coker, Ross Dobson, Amy Ruth Finegold,
Mat Follas, Vicky Jones, Jenny Linford,
Hannah Miles, Jane Montgomery, Fiona
Smith, Milli Taylor, Jenna Zoe and Ryland,
Peters & Small 2017, 2020 (see right for
full recipe credits).
Design and photographs © Ryland Peters
& Small 2017, 2020 (see page 64 for full
image credits).

ISBN: 978-1-78879-195-3

10 9 8 7 6 5 4 3 2 1

Printed in China

NOTES

• Both British (Metric) and American (Imperial plus
US cup) measurements are included in these recipes
for your convenience, however it is important to work
with one set of measurements only and not alternate
between the two within a recipe.

• All spoon measurements are level unless otherwise
specified.

• All eggs are medium (UK) or large (US), unless
otherwise specified. Uncooked or partially cooked
eggs should not be served to the very old, frail, young
children, pregnant women or those with
compromised immune systems.

• When a recipe calls for the grated zest of citrus
fruit, buy unwaxed fruit and wash well before using.
If you can only find treated fruit, scrub well in warm
soapy water before using.

• Ovens should be preheated to the specified
temperatures. We recommend using an oven
thermometer. If using a fan-assisted oven, adjust
temperatures according to the manufacturer's
instructions.

RECIPE CREDITS

Hannah Miles
Black bean dip with blue corn
  chips
Blue cheese & walnut dip
Buffalo chicken wing dip
Creamy cashew & roasted tomato
  dip
French onion dip
Hawaiian-style bacon & pineapple
  dip
Hot philly steak dip
Layered "nacho" dip with tortilla
  chips
Maryland crab dip
Pea feta & fresh mint dip
Peanut satay dip
Ranch dip with baked sweet potato
  chips
Smoked salmon, horseradish & dill
  dip with bagel toasts
Spicy beer mustard dip with
  maple-glazed sausages
Warm olive and artichoke dip

Milli Taylor
Beetroot hummus with squid ink
  crackers
Creamy artichoke & spinach dip
Cucumber and mint tzatziki
Marinated feta dip
Roast carrot, ginger & miso dip
Romesco dip with grilled spring
  onions/scallions

Fiona Smith
Artichoke tarator
Griddled vegetable hummus
Macadamia & chilli dip
Minted pea or bean hummus
Roast garlic hummus

Jenny Linford
Broad/fava bean & ricotta dip
Classic hummus
Roast garlic herbed labneh
Roasted red pepper raita

Jenna Zoe
Lighter guacamole
Zesty almond & herb pesto
Edamame & wasabi dip

**Chloe Coker and
Jane Montgomery**
Baba ghanoush with paprika pitta
  chips
Sweet potato hummus with herby
  breadsticks

Mat Follas
Truffled cauliflower dip

Ross Dobson
Muhammara

Jordan Bourke
Dukkah

Amy Ruth Finegold
White bean & spinach dip with
  wholewheat crostini

Vicky Jones
Fava & chicory/endive dip

Ghillie Başan
Labneh with dried & fresh mint
Labneh with harissa, coriander/
  cilantro & honey

Ryland Peters & Small
Tuna melt dip
Tapenade
Labneh with garlic, red chillies/
  chiles & dill

CONTENTS

INTRODUCTION

Who doesn't enjoy a delicious dip? The ultimate in food for sharing, dips are most often enjoyed at social gatherings – from drinks or a movie night in with a few friends to celebratory parties and special occasion buffets. Designed to be enjoyed from a communal bowl, dips can be paired with dippers to create customized bites to suit every taste and are often eaten with one hand, leaving the other hand free to cope with a glass of wine! Here are some simple guidelines to successful dip service:

Season with care. Although it's usual to season to taste during preparation, it's best to check the seasoning of your dip with your intended dipper. Salted or peppered breadsticks or crackers may mean that less seasoning is required in the dip itself. Likewise if you are serving a dip with very bland dippers, the dip needs to be full of flavour and bordering on over-seasoned. A squeeze of lemon juice or a splash of wine vinegar can often give a dip the lift it needs at the last minute.

Allow time. Where possible avoid serving your dips straight from the fridge. Giving them a little time to come to room temperature will mean they are a better dipping consistency and have a fuller flavour. Hot dips should be served hot, of course, but not dangerously so. Always carefully check the temperature of a hot dip yourself before serving to others.

Presentation matters. Garnishing your dips creatively can make them more appealing as well as hint at the flavours contained within. Reserve a sprig of fresh herbs, a few jewel-bright edamame beans or pomegranate seeds; add a scattering of toasted pine nuts or sesame seeds; a dusting of paprika for colour contrast or a slick of good quality olive oil, balsamic glaze or pomegranate molasses can look very attractive. Always add your garnish just before serving.

PERFECT PAIRINGS – WHICH DIPPERS TO CHOOSE?

Crisps/chips Potato crisps/chips have a deliciously crunchy texture and are often quite resilient. Choose from the numerous potato, root vegetable, corn, rice, pitta or bagel products available in stores or make your own using the recipes provided in this book. Try and flavour-match your chips and dips

sympathetically – for example, sweet potato chips work well with cool, creamy dips; salty potato chips are good with rich, cheesy dips; or use simple pitta with spiced dips, etc. If unsure, it's best to stick to plain or salted varieties to avoid any flavour clashes.

Crackers Seeded and whole-grain crackers are good all-rounders but work particularly well with bean and pulse-based dips as their nuttiness complements both the earthy flavour and texture of these wholesome dips.

Crudités Batons and strips of crisp vegetables are a healthy and colourful choice. Choose from raw carrots, celery, sweet peppers, cucumbers, radishes and chicory/endive leaves to create a classic selection. If you want to add interest, you can also use baby corn, asparagus spears, sugar snap peas, broccoli and cauliflower florets, but these are all best if blanched for just a minute or two before serving.

Bread Soft, fresh bread is good for absorbing light dips. Cubes of focaccia and slices of fresh baguette/French stick work well. Middle-eastern style breads such as pitta and lavash are better sliced into strips and lightly toasted to give them a firmer texture. Ditto for oven-baked crostini toasts, which make excellent crispy dippers. A good tip is to buy part-baked baguettes/French sticks which are easier to slice very thinly. Then simply brush your slices on both sides with olive oil and bake on a tray in an oven preheated to 180°C (350°F) Gas 4 for 8–10 minutes until light brown and crispy. Crostini also have the advantage of keeping in an airtight container for up to 5 days, so can be made in batches in advance and stored.

CHAPTER 1

MEAT, POULTRY & FISH

SPICY BEER MUSTARD DIP
WITH MAPLE-GLAZED SAUSAGES

This delicious mustard dip is classically served with soft pretzels or sausages. Here it's paired with little cocktail sausages which are the ideal size for dipping! Making your own mustard is easy, although you will need to soak the mustard seeds overnight.

FOR THE SPICY BEER MUSTARD DIP
80 g/3 oz. yellow mustard seeds
25 g/1 oz. black mustard seeds
125 ml/½ cup strong beer
125 ml/½ cup cider vinegar
80 g/½ cup soft dark brown sugar
40 ml/2½ tablespoons maple syrup
1 teaspoon ground allspice
1 tablespoon creamed horseradish
salt and black pepper

FOR THE MAPLE-GLAZED SAUSAGES
24 mini sausages or 12 chipolatas
12 rashers/slices streaky bacon
a little olive oil
3 tablespoons maple syrup
1 tablespoon sesame seeds

Cocktail sticks/toothpicks

Serves 6–8

Put the yellow and black mustard seeds in a bowl and pour over the beer and cider vinegar. Cover the bowl with clingfilm/plastic wrap and put in the refrigerator overnight to soak. The mustard seeds will absorb some of the liquid and become soft. The following day, put the soaked seeds and soaking liquor into a food processor or blender with the sugar, maple syrup, ground allspice and creamed horseradish and blitz for a few minutes until smooth. It will still have some small pieces of mustard seed which give a great texture to the dip. Season with salt and pepper to your taste. This recipe makes plenty of mustard so you may want to reserve half in a sealed sterilized jar and keep it in the refrigerator.

For the sausages, preheat the oven to 180°C (350°F) Gas 4.

If using chipolatas, twist the centre of each sausage then cut with scissors to make 24 mini sausages. Cut the bacon strips in half, wrap one half strip around each mini sausage and secure in place with a cocktail stick/toothpick. Put in a roasting pan and drizzle with a little olive oil and roast in the preheated oven for 25–30 minutes until the sausages turn golden brown. Drizzle with the maple syrup, sprinkle with the sesame seeds and bake for a further 5 minutes. Serve the sausages hot or cold with the spicy beer mustard dip.

HAWAIIAN-STYLE BACON & PINEAPPLE DIP

This decadent hot dip is made with gooey melted cheese, pineapple and salty pancetta. You can replace the pancetta with ready-cooked ham or fried bacon lardons if you prefer. Or, if pepperoni pizza is your favourite, try swapping the pancetta for pepperoni slices. I like to use fresh pineapple as it has more flavour but canned pineapple is also fine to use and is quicker to prepare.

100 g/3½ oz. pancetta rashers/ slices

4 slices of fresh pineapple or 4 canned pineapple rings

250 g/9 oz. cream cheese

125 ml/½ cup your favourite Thousand Island dressing

1 tablespoon sun-dried tomato purée/paste

100 g/3½ oz. Red Leicester or Colby cheese, grated/shredded

salt and freshly ground black pepper

Tortilla Chips (page 40) or crusty bread to serve

Serves 6–8

Preheat the oven to 180°C (350°F) Gas 4.

Chop the strips of pancetta into about 3-cm/1-in. pieces and put in the roasting pan. If using a fresh pineapple, remove the skin, eyes and hard core, then chop into small pieces. If using tinned/canned pineapple, chop the rings into small pieces. Add the pineapple to the roasting pan and bake in the hot oven for 10 minutes. Remove from the oven and leave to cool slightly.

Put the cream cheese in a mixing bowl. Add the Thousand Island dressing and tomato purée and whisk together until smooth. Stir in the grated cheese, cooled pancetta and pineapple pieces, and season with salt and pepper. Bake in the oven for 20–25 minutes until golden brown on top. Leave to cool slightly for about 10 minutes then serve warm with tortilla chips or crusty bread for dipping.

Variation Hawaiian "pizza" dip Try using pepperoni slices instead of the pancetta and arrange them on top of the dip as you would with a pizza. This cute novelty presentation is guaranteed to appeal to the kids! To reinforce the theme, you can serve it with a pizza dough base, cut into wedges for dipping.

HOT PHILLY STEAK DIP

This recipe is inspired by one of the most popular steak recipes in America – a Philly cheesesteak – a steak sandwich made with thin slices of beef, topped with melting cheese. Dip in tortilla chips or crusty bread while watching the Super Bowl.

1 green (bell) pepper

1 medium onion

1 tablespoon olive oil

1 teaspoon balsamic glaze or vinegar

1 teaspoon caster/granulated white sugar

salt and freshly ground black pepper

6 slices roast beef

250 g/9 oz. cream cheese

125 ml/½ cup your favourite ranch salad dressing

1 tablespoon creamed horseradish

100 g/3½ oz. provolone or cheddar cheese, grated/shredded

Tortilla Chips (page 40) or crusty bread, to serve

Serves 6–8

Preheat the oven to 180°C (350°F) Gas 4.

Cut away the top of the (bell) pepper and discard. Cut the pepper in half, remove all of the seeds, then cut into small chunks about 1-cm/⅜-in. diameter. Peel and finely chop the onion. Put the peppers and onion in a large frying pan/skillet with the olive oil and fry over a gentle heat until the onions and peppers are soft and the onion starts to caramelize. Drizzle with the balsamic, sprinkle over the caster/granulated sugar, season with salt and pepper and fry/sauté for a few more minutes.

Cut the roast beef into small pieces and add to the pan. Cook for a minute or so, so that the meat absorbs the flavours from the pan. Remove from the heat and leave to cool for a few minutes.

In a mixing bowl whisk together the cream cheese, ranch dressing and creamed horseradish. Fold the grated cheese into the mixture with the beef and vegetables.

Bake in the preheated oven for 20–25 minutes until the cheese has melted and the top of the dip has started to turn light golden brown. Leave to cool for about 10 minutes before serving as the dip should be served warm and not hot. Serve with tortilla chips or small slices of crusty bread for dipping. Delicious!

Variation Spicy hot Philly dip To make a spicy version fold in some finely chopped jarred jalapeños with the beef before baking.

HOT BUFFALO CHICKEN WING DIP

This dip has the taste of hot buffalo wings but without the bother of getting messy fingers eating actual wings. Hot sauces vary considerably in fierceness so please do add gradually and taste to ensure that you don't end up with a dip that is too hot to eat, because that would be a travesty!

300 g/10½ oz. cream cheese

170 ml/¾ cup ranch salad dressing

125 ml/½ cup red hot chilli sauce (such as Frank's)

150 g/5½ oz. cheddar cheese, grated/shredded

200 g/7 oz. cooked chicken breast

freshly ground black pepper

Tortilla Chips (page 40), to serve

Serves 6–8

Preheat the oven to 180°C (350°F) Gas 4.

Put the cream cheese, ranch dressing and hot sauce in a bowl and whisk together until smooth. Stir in the grated cheese. Remove any skin from the chicken breasts and discard, then chop into small pieces and stir into the sauce. Season with cracked black pepper and taste. You can add a little salt if you wish, but there should be sufficient salt from the dressing and hot sauce.

Bake in the oven for 25–30 minutes until the top of the dip starts to turn light golden brown. Remove from the heat and leave to cool for a short while then serve warm with tortilla chips.

Variation Vegetarian buffalo chicken wing dip To make a version suitable for vegetarians to enjoy, simply use a vegetarian cheese and replace the cooked chicken breast with butter/lima beans or small florets of steamed or boiled cauliflower.

MARYLAND CRAB DIP

150 g/5½ oz. cream cheese

125 ml/½ cup buttermilk

2 tablespoons mayonnaise

1 tablespoon hot chilli sauce
(such as Frank's)

freshly ground black pepper

freshly squeezed juice of 1 lemon

120 g/4½ oz. cheddar or provolone,
grated/shredded

100 g/3½ oz. white or brown
crabmeat

a pinch of ground chilli/chili pepper

3 tablespoons panko breadcrumbs

celery sticks, to serve

Serves 6–8

**A rich and creamy dip with mild spicy heat.
For a twist, fold in chopped lobster or shrimp
in place of the crab.**

Preheat the oven to 180°C (350°F) Gas 4.

Place the cream cheese, buttermilk and mayonnaise in a
bowl and whisk together until smooth. Add the hot sauce,
a grind of black pepper and lemon juice, and whisk to
combine. Divide the grated cheese into ⅔ and ⅓. Add the
larger portion to the mix with the crabmeat and chilli/chili
pepper, and fold together gently until mixed. Spoon into an
ovenproof bowl. Cover the top with the remaining cheese
and sprinkle over the panko breadcrumbs.

Bake in the preheated oven for 20–25 minutes until the
cheese on top is golden brown. Remove from the oven and
leave to cool for 10 minutes before serving with celery sticks
and tortilla chips for dipping.

TUNA MELT DIP

225 g/8 oz. cream cheese

2 tablespoons butter, softened

2 tablespoons mayonnaise

65 ml/½ cup sour cream

2 tablespoons freshly squeezed
lemon juice

1–2 tablespoons very finely diced
spring onions/scallions

2 tablespoons chopped flat-leaf
parsley

½ teaspoon paprika

¼ teaspoon ground black pepper

2 x 400-g/14 oz. cans tuna, drained

50 g/½ cup grated/shredded
cheddar

Potato Crisps/Chips (page 63),
to serve

Serves 6–8

**The tried-and-tested combination of tuna and
melted cheddar creates a hot dip that's sure to
become a family favourite.**

Preheat oven to 180°C (350°F) Gas 4.

Blend the softened cream cheese with the softened butter.
Blend in the mayonnaise and sour cream until smooth. Add
the lemon juice, spring onion/scallion, parsley, salt and
pepper. Stir in the flaked, well-drained tuna and cheese.

Bake in the preheated oven for 10–15 minutes, until hot
and bubbly. Remove from the oven and leave to cool for
10 minutes before serving with potato crisps/chips.

SMOKED SALMON, HORSERADISH & DILL DIP WITH BAGEL TOASTS

Salmon and horseradish are a match made in heaven and pair perfectly in this creamy dip. You can adjust the lemon to your taste adding a little more for a really zingy flavour. Bagel toasts work really well and are so simple to make, there's no comparison between shop-bought and homemade.

200 g/7 oz. smoked salmon slices

freshly squeezed juice of 1 lemon

250 ml/1 cup crème fraîche or sour cream

1 tablespoon fresh dill, chopped, plus extra to serve

125 g/4½ oz. cream cheese

1 tablespoon creamed horseradish

freshly ground black pepper

FOR THE BAGEL TOASTS

3 plain bagels, stale is fine!

3 tablespoons olive oil

1 tablespoon poppy seeds or sesame seeds (optional)

Serves 4

Reserve a piece of smoked salmon for garnish then blitz the rest into small pieces in a food processor or blender with the lemon juice. Add the crème fraîche, dill, cream cheese and creamed horseradish and season with freshly ground black pepper. Smoked salmon is quite salty so you shouldn't need to add salt. Blitz for a few seconds until everything is combined. Spoon into a bowl and garnish with the reserved salmon and a little sprig of dill.

For the bagel toasts, preheat the grill/broiler to hot.

Using a sharp knife, slice each bagel horizontally into 4 and arrange the thin slices on the grill pan. Grill on one side until lightly browned then remove from the oven and turn over. Brush the oil over the untoasted side of the bagels. Scatter over the seeds, if using, and return to the grill/broiler. Toast until crisp and golden. Serve immediately or let cool and store in an airtight container for up to 2 days.

Serve the dip with the warm bagel toasts on the side.

Variation Smoked salmon, caper and red onion dip
Try replacing the dill and horseradish with a few spoonfuls of drained and chopped capers and some very finely chopped red onion.

CHAPTER 2

PEAS, BEANS & LEGUMES

BLACK BEAN DIP WITH BLUE CORN CHIPS

Black beans are very popular in Mexican cookery and here they are used to make a spicy dip which has a fresh taste of lime, coriander/cilantro and tomato. Serve with freshly made blue corn chips.

230 g/½ lb. cooked black beans, drained weight

2 spring onions/scallions, trimmed

freshly squeezed juice of 2 limes

15 g/½ oz. fresh coriander/cilantro, plus extra to serve

100 g/3½ oz. block of creamed coconut

1–2 red chillies/chiles, depending on heat required, deseeded

1 teaspoon soft dark brown sugar

salt and pepper

2 tablespoons plain yogurt

10 cherry tomatoes

olive oil, to drizzle

FOR THE BLUE CORN CHIPS

8 soft blue corn tortillas

salt

Serves 6–8

Drain the black beans in a sieve/strainer and rinse under cold water. Reserve a spoonful of the beans for garnish then put the rest in a food processor or blender with the trimmed spring onions/scallions, lime juice, coriander/cilantro, creamed coconut, chillies/chiles and sugar and blitz until smooth. Season with salt and pepper to taste. Add 2–3 spoonfuls of yogurt to loosen the dip as required.

Deseed the tomatoes and chop into small pieces. Reserve a spoonful of the chopped tomatoes for garnish, then fold the rest into the dip.

To make the blue corn chips, preheat the oven to 200°C (400°F) Gas 6. Stack the tortillas and using a sharp knife or scissors cut them into even-sized triangles – you can choose the size you want!

Spread them out in a single layer on a 2 baking sheets, spacing them at least 5 mm/¼-in. apart. Shake salt over them. Bake in the preheated oven for 8–12 minutes until starting to get crispy and slightly golden brown at the edges.

Spoon the dip into a serving bowl and top with the reserved tomato and beans and garnish with a little extra fresh coriander/cilantro. Drizzle with a little olive oil and serve with the blue corn chips.

CLASSIC HUMMUS

This hugely popular tasty, nutty-flavoured Middle Eastern dip is so easy to make at home. Serve it with pitta bread, falafel or vegetable crudités as a snack or alongside other mezze dishes for a light meal.

125 g/¾ cup dried chickpeas/
    garbanzo beans

1 teaspoon bicarbonate of soda/
    baking soda

salt

2 garlic cloves, peeled and crushed
    to a paste in a mortar with a pestle

4 tablespoons tahini

freshly squeezed juice of 1 lemon

toasted or griddled pitta bread,
    to serve

TO GARNISH

extra virgin olive oil

paprika or sumac

finely chopped flat-leaf parsley

Serves 6

Soak the chickpeas/garbanzo beans overnight in plenty of cold water with the bicarbonate of soda/baking soda.

Next day, drain and rinse. Put in a large pan, add enough fresh cold water to cover well and bring to the boil. Reduce the heat and simmer for 50–60 minutes until tender, skimming off any scum. Season the chickpeas with salt, then drain, reserving the cooking water and setting aside 1 tablespoon of the cooked chickpeas/garbanzo beans for the garnish.

In a food processor, blend together the cooked chickpeas/garbanzo beans, garlic, tahini and lemon juice. Gradually add in the cooking liquid until the mixture becomes a smooth paste. Season with salt.

Transfer the hummus to a serving bowl. To serve, make a shallow hollow in the centre using the back of a spoon. Pour in a little olive oil, top with the reserved whole chickpeas/garbanzo beans, a sprinkle of paprika or sumac and the chopped parsley. Serve with toasted or griddled pitta bread.

Variations

Roast garlic hummus Preheat the oven to 180°C (350°F) Gas 4. Cut about 1-cm/⅜-in. off the top of a whole bulb of garlic and discard. Loosely wrap the garlic in foil and roast in the preheated oven for about 45 minutes until very soft. Let cool. Squeeze the soft garlic cloves out of their skins and add to the chickpeas when you blend them.

Griddled vegetable hummus On a barbecue or in a griddle/grill pan, cook slices of sweet red or yellow (bell) pepper, aubergine/eggplant and/or courgette/zucchini that have been tossed with a little olive oil. Add to the chickpeas when you blend them.

Minted pea or bean hummus Add 130 g/4½ oz. cooked peas or cooked and shelled broad beans/fava beans and 2 tablespoons chopped fresh mint to the chickpeas/garbanzo beans when you blend them. Garnish with mint instead of the flat-leaf parsley.

SWEET POTATO HUMMUS
WITH HERBY BREADSTICKS

This velvety smooth sweet potato hummus dip makes an interesting change from the more familiar chickpea-only version. The herby breadsticks are surprisingly simple to make and their crunchy texture makes them the perfect accompaniment here.

1 sweet potato, unpeeled

3 garlic cloves, unpeeled

½ x 400-g/14-oz. can of chickpeas/garbanzos

1 fresh red chilli/chile, finely chopped

a handful of fresh coriander/ cilantro leaves, chopped

2 tablespoons olive oil

grated zest and freshly squeezed juice of ½ a lime

salt and freshly ground black pepper

FOR THE HERBY BREADSTICKS

300 g/2¼ cups plain/all-purpose flour

2 teaspoons fast-action yeast

2 teaspoons salt

1 teaspoon sugar

4 tablespoons/¼ cup olive oil

120–150 ml/½–⅔ cup lukewarm water

a pinch of mixed dried herbs

a pinch of cayenne pepper

salt and freshly ground black pepper

Serves 4–6

Preheat the oven to 180°C (350°F) Gas 4. Roast the sweet potato in a roasting pan for 30–40 minutes until very soft. Add the garlic cloves to the pan about 20 minutes before the end of the cooking time. Remove from the oven and, when cool enough to handle, remove and discard the skins from the sweet potato and garlic cloves. Put in a food processor along with the chickpeas, chilli/chile, coriander/cilantro, olive oil and lime zest and blitz until it reaches the desired consistency. Season with salt, pepper and lime juice to taste.

To make the breadsticks, preheat the oven to 170°C (325°F) Gas 3. Combine the flour, yeast, salt and sugar in a bowl. Make a well in the centre, pour in the olive oil and water, and stir until well combined and the dough comes together. It should be soft but not sticky.

Knead the dough for 10 minutes by hand, cover with oiled clingfilm/plastic wrap or a damp cloth and leave it to rise in a warm place for 40 minutes–1 hour, or until doubled in size.

Divide the dough in half and keep half wrapped up so that it does not dry out. Roll half the dough out into a flat rectangle about 5 mm–1 cm/¼–⅜ in. thick, then cut it into 1-cm/ ⅜-in.-wide strips. Roll the strips into pencil-width tubes. Repeat with the other half of the dough. Spread the mixed dried herbs, cayenne pepper and salt and pepper on a board, then roll the breadsticks in them and put them on a floured baking sheet. Bake in the preheated oven for 20–30 minutes until golden. Remove from the oven and let cool on a wire rack.

When ready to serve, spoon the sweet potato hummus into a serving bowl and serve with the cooled breadsticks.

BEETROOT HUMMUS
WITH SQUID INK CRACKERS

This is a sophisticated dip and dipper combination that's sure to wow party guests. The rich red of the beetroot/beet hummus works beautifully with the dramatic black of the squid ink crackers and the slightly sweet and salty flavour combination is stunning. The ink is available in convenient sachets from Italian and Spanish specialist stores, and from some online retailers.

140 g/1 cup canned chickpeas/
  garbanzos, drained and rinsed

250 g/2 scant cups beetroot/beets,
  cooked and cubed

1 large garlic clove, peeled

2 tablespoons olive oil

1 tablespoon freshly squeezed
  lemon juice

2 tablespoons tahini

2–3 pinches of sea salt flakes

micro herbs such as pea shoots,
  to garnish

FOR THE SQUID INK CRACKERS

300 g/2¼ cups plain/all-purpose
  flour

1 teaspoon baking powder

1 teaspoon salt

½ teaspoon cayenne pepper

80 ml/⅓ cup olive oil

3 x 4 g/⅙ oz. squid ink sachets

Serves 4–6

To make the hummus, put all of the ingredients in a food processor or blender and blitz until smooth. Taste and adjust the seasoning, if necessary.

To make the crackers, preheat the oven to 180°C (350°F) Gas 4.

Mix the flour, baking powder, salt and cayenne pepper in a large mixing bowl, and make a well in the middle. Mix 150 ml/⅔ cup water with the olive oil and squid ink, then add to the well. Stir gently, slowly incorporating the dry ingredients until a dough forms.

Turn out the dough onto a floured surface, and knead for about 3–5 minutes, or until smooth. Divide the dough into 15 pieces and roll them into the desired shapes with a rolling pin.

Transfer the shapes to a baking sheet lined with baking parchment and bake for about 10–15 minutes in the preheated oven, or until crisp on the undersides. Cool on a wire rack. Keep in an airtight container for up to 3 days before serving.

Spoon the hummus into a bowl, garnish with a few pea shoots and serve with the squid ink crackers for dipping.

WHITE BEAN & SPINACH DIP
WITH WHOLEWHEAT CROSTINI

410 g/2½ cups white beans

freshly squeezed juice of 1 lemon

freshly squeezed juice of 1 small
orange

1 garlic clove, peeled

50 g/2 oz. fresh spinach leaves

3 tablespoons flaxseed oil

salt and freshly ground black pepper

FOR THE CROSTINI

2 wholemeal/wholewheat baguettes/
French sticks, each sliced into
30–35 slices about 5 mm/¼-in.
thick

100 ml/scant ½ cup olive oil

Serves 4–6

This is a beautifully, light and nutritious green dip that looks great garnished with fresh herbs. Serve with crunchy crostini.

Blend all of the dip ingredients except the spinach together in a food processor until blended but still chunky in texture. Coarsely chop the spinach and stir into the dip mixture. Season to taste with salt and freshly ground pepper.

To make the crostini, heat a griddle pan on high and brush each side of the bread with olive oil. Cook the bread, in batches, for 1 minute on each side, until the bread is toasted and crisp. Remove and put onto a wire rack to cool. Alternatively, bake them on a baking sheet in an oven at 180°C (350°F) Gas 4 for 8–10 minutes.

Spoon the dip into a bowl and serve with the crostini on the side.

EDAMAME & WASABI DIP

200 g/1½ cups shelled edamame
beans (fresh, or frozen and
thawed)

3 tablespoons sweet white miso
paste

1 tablespoon extra virgin olive oil

1 tablespoon tamari soy sauce

1 teaspoon wasabi paste

crudités or breadsticks, to serve

Serves 2–3

Edamame (soy) beans are a rare plant source of Omega-3 fatty acids so this delicious green dip packs a nutritional punch as well as making a lighter alternative to hummus.

Put most of the edamame beans (reserving some to garnish) and 1 tablespoon water in a food processor and blitz until smooth. Add the remaining ingredients and mix well so that everything is well incorporated.

Spoon into a bowl, top with the reserved edamame beans and serve with crudités or breadsticks.

BROAD/FAVA BEAN & RICOTTA DIP

250 g/9 oz. fresh or frozen broad/
   fava beans

2 garlic cloves, peeled and mashed

1 tablespoon olive oil

100 g/½ cup ricotta cheese

2 tablespoons chopped fresh dill,
   plus extra to garnish

salt and freshly ground black pepper

toasted pitta bread or crudités,
   to serve

Serves 4

A fresh-tasting dip, with a pleasant nutty flavour. Serve with strips of warm toasted pitta bread or crudités.

Preheat the oven to 180°C (350°F) Gas 4.

Cook the beans in a saucepan of boiling water until just tender. Drain, cool and pop the beans out of their skins.

Put the skinned beans, garlic and olive oil in a food processor and blend together; alternatively mash together in a bowl using a fork. Add in the ricotta, chopped dill, salt and pepper and blend together briefly.

Spoon into a bowl, garnish with dill fronds and serve with warm toasted pitta bread.

CREAMY FAVA & CHICORY DIP

250 g/1⅓ cups split dried fava
   beans

1 medium potato, peeled and diced

100 ml/½ cup olive oil, plus extra
   for frying

500 g/1 lb. chicory/endive

2 garlic cloves, crushed

salt

extra virgin olive oil, to drizzle

toasted sourdough bread, to serve

Serves 4–6

This soft, creamy mixture of puréed dried broad/fava beans is found in Puglia, southern Italy, where it is called 'ncapriata or fave e cicoria. A similar dish, macco, is served in Sicily, where it is often mixed with wild fennel. The dip itself is made from dried broad/fava beans that are already shelled.

In a large saucepan, boil the beans and potato in enough water to cover the beans by 4 cm/2 in. for about 1 hour. Add more boiling water during cooking if the mixture gets too dry. By the time the beans are cooked, most of the water should have been absorbed. Beat in the olive oil until you have a thick, smooth purée, then season well with salt.

Meanwhile, boil or steam the chicory/endive. While cooking, heat a tablespoon of olive oil in a frying pan/skillet, and gently sauté the garlic, then toss the drained chicory/endive in the garlicky oil.

To serve, spoon the dip into a bowl, drizzle with good olive oil and serve with slices of toasted sourdough bread.

CHAPTER 3

VEGETABLES & HERBS

BABA GHANOUSH WITH PAPRIKA PITTA CHIPS

Serve this Middle Eastern-style dip with smoked paprika-dusted pitta chips as a vegetarian appetizer, or with other dishes, such as Classic Hummus (page 23) or Cucumber & Mint Tzatziki (page 39), as part of a mezze spread.

2 aubergines/eggplants

2 garlic cloves, peeled

salt

freshly squeezed juice of ½ lemon

3 tablespoons extra virgin olive oil, plus extra to serve

pomegranate seeds, to garnish (optional)

FOR THE PAPRIKA PITTA CHIPS

2 tablespoons olive oil

1 tablespoon smoked paprika

salt and freshly ground black pepper

5 white pitta breads, halved lengthways and cut into strips

Serves 4–6

Preheat the oven to 200°C (400°F) Gas 6.

Put the aubergines/eggplants on a foil-lined baking sheet and roast in the preheated oven for 1 hour, turning over halfway through, until charred on all sides. Put the hot aubergines/eggplants in a plastic bag (so that the resulting steam will make the skin easier to peel off) and set aside.

Once cool, peel the roasted aubergines/eggplants and chop the flesh into chunks. Pound the garlic in a mortar with a pestle (with a pinch of salt) until it is a paste.

In a food processor, blend the roast aubergines/eggplants, garlic paste, lemon juice and olive oil to a smooth purée. Season with salt and cover until ready to serve.

To make the paprika pitta chips, turn the oven up to 200°C (400°F) Gas 6. Drizzle another foil-lined baking sheet with olive oil then sprinkle over the paprika and some salt and pepper. Put the pitta bread strips on the baking sheet and mix to coat. Bake in the oven for 8 minutes until slightly coloured and crisp.

Put the dip in a serving bowl and sprinkle with pomegranate seeds, if using. Drizzle with extra virgin olive oil and serve with the paprika pitta chips on the side for dipping.

TRUFFLED CAULIFLOWER DIP

½ a head of cauliflower, chopped into 1-cm/⅜-in. pieces

vegetable oil

salt

3 tablespoons double/heavy cream or dairy-free substitute if preferred

1 teaspoon truffle oil

6–8 slices thinly sliced toasted sourdough bread, to serve

Serves 4

Cauliflower is a hugely versatile and often underrated vegetable. Roasting gives it a delicious nuttiness that balances well here with the richness of truffle oil to make a velvety and indulgent dip.

Preheat the oven to 180°C (350°F) Gas 4.

Put the cauliflower in a saucepan, cover with water and set over a low–medium heat. Simmer for 5 minutes, then drain and scatter onto a baking sheet. Drizzle with a little vegetable oil and sprinkle with salt. Roast in the preheated oven for 10–12 minutes until just starting to turn golden.

Remove from the oven and return to the saucepan. Add the cream and a pinch of salt. Purée using a handheld electric blender (or in a blender) until it resembles cottage cheese. Set aside to cool, then put in the refrigerator. Once it has cooled completely, stir in the truffle oil. Serve at room temperature with the toasted sourdough.

CREAMY ARTICHOKE & SPINACH DIP

80 g/3 oz. fresh baby spinach leaves, washed and stalks removed

1 x 280-g/10-oz. jar chargrilled artichoke hearts in oil (170 g/6 oz. drained weight)

20 g/¾ oz. garlic and herb soft cheese (such as Boursin)

40 g/1½ oz. Parmesan cheese, grated

80 g/3 oz. sour cream or crème fraîche

salt and freshly ground black pepper

crostini or thinly sliced toasted sourdough bread, to serve

Serves 4

This delicious dip can be prepared in a matter of minutes. Using a garlic and herb soft cheese adds instant depth of flavour but if preferred you can substitute with a plain cream cheese and add any finely chopped fresh green herb – basil works well.

Blitz the spinach in a food processor or blender.

Drain the artichoke hearts, roughly chop and add to the food processor or blender with all the remaining ingredients. Blitz until smooth then season to taste with salt and freshly ground black pepper.

Serve slightly chilled with crostini or toasted sourdough, as preferred.

ZESTY ALMOND & HERB PESTO

20 g/¾ oz. fresh baby spinach leaves

leaves from 1 small bunch each fresh mint, flat-leaf parsley and coriander/cilantro

30 g/¼ cup blanched almonds

6 tablespoons extra virgin olive oil, plus extra to preserve

1 kaffir lime leaf

freshly squeezed juice of 1 lime

grated zest of 1 lemon

1 garlic clove, peeled

a pinch of sea salt

crudités or breadsticks, to serve

Serves 2

Traditionally pesto is made with basil, pine nuts and Parmesan but this cheese-free version is made with a mixture of fresh green herbs and almonds. The zesty flavour comes from the lemon zest and kaffir lime leaf. If you can't find kaffir lime, use lemongrass instead.

Put all the ingredients in a food processor and blitz until they form a paste.

Spoon into a dish and serve immediately with crudités, such as carrots and cucumber batons, or breadsticks, for dipping. (Be aware that the herbs will oxidize and the dip will loose it's vibrant green colour fairly quickly after making so it's important to serve it very fresh.)

LIGHTER GUACAMOLE

1 large avocado, stoned

90 g/3 oz. peas, ideally fresh, but frozen and thawed is fine too

½ red (bell) pepper, deseeded

2 tomatoes

¼ small onion

1 garlic clove, peeled

large handful of fresh coriander/cilantro

freshly squeezed juice of ½ lime

1 tablespoon freshly squeezed lemon juice, plus extra to preserve

crudités or breadsticks, to serve

Serves 2

Although traditional guacamole is made with fresh healthy ingredients, it does have a high calorie content. This version has been lightened up with the inclusion of fresh peas and (bell) peppers. It keeps it's creamy texture and body, but makes it a lighter option.

Put all the ingredients in a food processor and blitz until smooth.

Spoon into a dish and serve immediately with crudités, such as carrot batons, or breadsticks, for dipping. (Be aware that the avocado will quickly brown and the dip will loose it's vibrant green colour fairly quickly after making so it's important to serve it very fresh.)

ROAST CARROT, GINGER & MISO DIP

300 g/10½ oz. sweet carrots, peeled and thinly sliced

25 g/1 oz. grated fresh ginger

3 tablespoons white miso paste

2 tablespoons tahini

black and white sesame seeds, to garnish (optional)

Tortilla Chips (page 40) or crackers, to serve

Serves 4

Roasted carrots make a deliciously creamy and sweet dip. The ginger adds a welcome spicy heat and the miso (fermented soya bean paste) adds a moreish savoury note.

Preheat the oven to 180°C (350°F) Gas 4.

Put the carrots in a roasting pan and roast in the preheated oven for 20–25 minutes until softened but not browned. Set aside until cool.

Blitz the cooled carrots in a food processor or blender together with the ginger, miso and tahini.

Spoon into a bowl, garnish with a sprinkling of with sesame seeds, if using, and serve with homemade tortilla chips or plain crackers.

CUCUMBER & MINT TZATZIKI

1 large, firm cucumber

½ teaspoon salt plus 2 pinches

400 g/2 scant cups Greek/US strained plain yogurt

2 tablespoons freshly chopped dill, plus extra to garnish (optional)

2 garlic cloves, peeled and crushed

1 tablespoon olive oil

Squid Ink Crackers (page 27) or Tortilla Chips (page 40), to serve

Serves 4–6

A Greek classic, this creamy combination of yogurt, cucumber and fresh mint is so simple to make but uniquely refreshing.

Peel, deseed and dice the cucumber, reserve a little to garnish. Sprinkle the rest of it with ½ teaspoon salt, mix well and set aside for 5 minutes. Wrap the cucumber in a spotlessly clean kitchen towel and squeeze to remove the liquid.

Put in a bowl, reserving a few pieces to garnish, then add the remaining ingredients. Mix together well and serve, garnished with cucumber and dill, if you like.

Variations

Beetroot/beet tzatziki Add 1 medium raw grated beetroot/beet and 2 tablespoons chopped chives to the mixture.

Olive tzatziki Stir 100 g/¾–1 cup finely chopped pitted black or green olives into the cucumber and yogurt mixture.

LAYERED 'NACHO' DIP
WITH TORTILLA CHIPS

One of the all-time favourite sharing plates is nachos – tortilla chips are served piled high with tomato salsa, guacamole, sour cream and grated/shredded cheese then warmed under a grill. This dip version is layered up in a bowl and then warmed, ready to scoop out with crunchy homemade tortilla chips.

FOR THE GUACAMOLE

6 ripe hass/haas avocados, halved and pitted

½ red onion

a handful of freshly chopped coriander/cilantro

2 fresh red chillies/chiles, deseeded and finely chopped

freshly squeezed juice of 2 limes

2–3 pinches of sea salt flakes

Tabasco and cayenne pepper (optional), to taste

FOR THE TOMATO SALSA

6 ripe medium tomatoes

freshly squeezed juice of 1 lime

10g/⅓ oz. fresh coriander/cilantro

2 spring onions/scallions, trimmed

1 fresh red chilli/chile, trimmed and deseeded

salt and freshly ground black pepper

FOR THE TORTILLA CHIPS

8 small soft wheat flour tortillas

sunflower or vegetable oil

TO ASSEMBLE

200 ml/7 fl. oz. sour cream

125 g/4½ oz. strong cheese, such as mature/sharp cheddar, grated/shredded

a handful of jarred jalapeño slices (optional)

Serves 6

Scoop the flesh out of the avocados with a tablespoon into a shallow bowl. Add the onion, coriander/cilantro and chillies/chiles. Add the lime juice, then mash everything together with a fork, leaving the texture quite chunky. Season with salt to taste. Add a few dashes of Tabasco and a few pinches of cayenne, if using. Cover with clingfilm/plastic wrap until ready to use.

For the salsa, cut the tomatoes in half then scoop out and discard the seeds. Put in a blender or food processor along with the lime juice, coriander/cilantro, spring onions/scallions and chilli/chile and pulse for a few seconds to roughly chop the tomatoes. Season to taste with salt and pepper. Cover with clingfilm/plastic wrap until ready to use.

To make the fried tortilla chips, stack the tortillas and cut each one into 8 even triangles, like a pizza. Pour about 2.5 cm/1 in. oil into a small saucepan then put over a medium-high heat. When the oil is hot, test-fry one triangle – it should take about 30 seconds for the first side to become crisp. Using tongs or a slotted spoon, turn the tortilla over to fry the other side. Fry the remaining tortillas in batches and, when golden brown, drain on paper towels. When cool, store in an airtight container until ready to use.

To assemble the dip, spoon the guacamole into a shallow serving bowl and spread out in a thick layer. Top with the tomato salsa, then spoon over the sour cream, scatter over the grated cheese and finish with jalapeños, if using. Gently warm under a preheated grill/broiler just until the cheese starts to melt. Serve straight away with the tortilla chips.

CHAPTER 4

OLIVES, NUTS & SEEDS

CREAMY CASHEW & ROASTED TOMATO DIP

This dip has a wonderful nutty texture and the roasted tomatoes give it a sweet smoky flavour. This recipe needs some time to prepare as the cashews are best soaked in water overnight so that the dip is creamy.

200 g/7 oz. unsalted cashew nuts, soaked in a bowl of water overnight

250 g/9 oz. sweet cherry tomatoes

1 tablespoon olive oil, plus extra to serve

1 tablespoon balsamic glaze or good-quality balsamic vinegar

salt and freshly ground pepper

1 teaspoon caster/granulated sugar

2 large sprigs of fresh thyme

200 ml/7 fl. oz. buttermilk

freshly squeezed juice of 1 lemon

Pitta Chips (page 32) or crusty bread, to serve

Serves 4

Preheat the oven to 140°C (275°F) Gas 1.

Cut the tomatoes in half and put, cut-side up, on a roasting pan. Drizzle with the olive oil and balsamic glaze or vinegar and season well with salt and pepper. Sprinkle over the sugar. Pull the thyme sprigs between your fingers to remove the tiny leaves and sprinkle the leaves over the tomatoes. Roast the tomatoes in the oven for about 1½–2 hours, until almost dried but still a little soft. Remove from the oven and leave to cool.

Drain the cashews and discard the water. Put the nuts in a blender with the buttermilk, lemon juice and most of the roasted tomatoes, along with their juices. Reserve a few tomatoes for garnish.

Blitz to a smooth purée and taste for seasoning, adding salt, pepper or lemon juice to taste. Spoon into a bowl and top with the reserved roasted tomatoes and a drizzle of olive oil. Serve with pitta chips or slices of crusty bread for dipping.

PEANUT SATAY DIP

1 tablespoon soy or tamari sauce

1 tablespoon soft dark brown sugar

100-g/3½-oz. block creamed coconut

2 tablespoons crunchy peanut butter

150 g/5½ oz. cream cheese

freshly squeezed juice of 1 lime

2 tablespoons crème fraîche or sour cream

1 tablespoon roasted peanuts, finely chopped

coriander/cilantro leaves, to garnish

prawn/shrimp crackers or carrot batons, to serve

Serves 4–6

Peanut satay makes a great dip to serve as a snack before a Thai meal with prawn/shrimp crackers and carrot batons to dip. The recipe uses solid creamed coconut but you can substitute this for a small can of creamed coconut if you need to, though as it's runnier you may not need to add the crème fraîche.

In a bowl, whisk the soy sauce and brown sugar together until the sugar has dissolved. Put the mixture in a blender with the creamed coconut, peanut butter, cream cheese and lime juice and blitz until smooth. Fold through the crème fraîche to loosen.

Spoon into a bowl and garnish with chopped peanuts and coriander/cilantro leaves, if you like. Serve straight away with prawn/shrimp crackers and carrot batons, for dipping. (Be aware that if you chill the dip in the refrigerator it will set so you will need to bring it to room temperature again or heat gently before serving.)

MACADAMIA & CHILLI/CHILE DIP

1 tablespoon macadamia or groundnut oil

1 teaspoon blachan (Thai shrimp paste)

2 garlic cloves, peeled and crushed

4 shallots, finely chopped

125 ml/½ cup coconut cream

1 tablespoon brown sugar

70 g/2½ oz. cup macadamia nuts, toasted

3 large fresh red chillies/chiles, chopped

1 teaspoon finely chopped lemongrass

1 tablespoon soy sauce

Sweet Potato Chips (page 52), or crudités

Serves 2–3

This is a variation on a peanut satay dip. It's particularly good with Sweet Potato Chips (page 52) or it can be served with crudités.

Heat the oil in a small saucepan. Add the blachan and gently fry for 1 minute, breaking it up with a wooden spoon. Add the garlic and shallots and sauté for 3 minutes. Add the coconut cream and sugar and bring to the boil, then reduce to a simmer for 1 minute.

Put the macadamia nuts, chillies/chiles, lemongrass and soy sauce in a blender or small food processor and blend in bursts, adding the coconut cream mixture a little at a time until well combined.

Spoon the dip into a dish and serve with sweet potato chips or crudités, as preferred.

ROMESCO DIP WITH GRILLED
SPRING ONIONS/SCALLIONS

6 medium tomatoes, halved

4 red (bell) peppers, halved and deseeded

salt and freshly ground black pepper

8 tablespoons olive oil

50 g/generous ⅓ cup hazelnuts or almonds, blanched

15-cm/6-in. piece of stale white baguette/French bread, broken into chunks

3 garlic cloves, peeled

1 tablespoon sherry vinegar

½ teaspoon smoked paprika

12 spring onions/scallions, tops and bottoms trimmed

Serves 4–6

Romesco is a Spanish sauce traditionally served with grilled spring onions/scallions.

Preheat the oven to 200°C (400°F) Gas 6.

Put the tomatoes and peppers in separate roasting pans, season and drizzle 1 tablespoon of the olive oil over each. Roast in the oven for about 35 minutes, or until the pepper skins have started to blacken. Meanwhile, blitz the blanched nuts in a food processor or blender and leave them in there.

Remove the tomatoes from the pan and set aside. Add the chunks of baguette/French bread to the tomato juices in the pan. Let cool. Remove the peppers from the pan, put into a bowl, cover with clingfilm/plastic wrap and allow to cool. Once cooled, remove and discard the pepper skins and add the flesh to the food processor, along with the tomatoes. Add 4 tablespoons of the olive oil, along with the garlic, soaked bread, sherry vinegar and smoked paprika. Blitz until smooth.

To prepare the spring onions/scallions, preheat the grill/broiler to high. Drizzle the remaining olive oil over them and toss to coat. Arrange them on the grill pan and cook, turning, for 3–5 minutes. Serve warm with the romesco dip.

ARTICHOKE TARATOR

2 slices of day-old bread, crusts removed

6 canned artichoke hearts, drained

freshly squeezed juice of 1 lemon

3–4 garlic cloves, peeled and crushed

½ teaspoon salt

70 g/2½ oz. blanched almonds, finely chopped

4 tablespoons olive oil, plus extra to serve

toasted flaked/slivered almonds, to garnish

endive/chicory or bread cubes, to serve

Serves 2–3

Tarator is a tasty Turkish garlic and nut dip, and this version has artichokes to make it extra special. Perfect as a dip with vegetable crudités – it goes especially well with the bitterness of chicory/endive.

Put the bread in a sieve/strainer and pour over boiling water; when cool enough to handle, squeeze out any excess water.

Chop the artichoke hearts and put in a food processor with the bread, lemon juice, garlic, salt and almonds. Blend together, adding the oil slowly to combine.

Spoon into a bowl, drizzle with extra oil and scatter with the flaked/slivered almonds. Serve with endive/chicory leaves for scooping, or cubes of bread, as preferred.

MUHAMMARA

3 large red (bell) peppers

1 slice of day-old sourdough bread, cut into small pieces

100 g/3½ oz. walnut halves, coarsely chopped

½ teaspoon dried red chilli/hot pepper flakes

1 tablespoon sun-dried tomato paste

2 garlic cloves, peeled and chopped

2 teaspoons freshly squeezed lemon juice

1 tablespoon balsamic vinegar

2 teaspoons caster/granulated sugar

1 teaspoon ground cumin

2 tablespoons olive oil, plus extra to serve

chopped pistachios, to serve

sea salt and freshly ground black pepper

toasted pitta or other flatbread, to serve

Serves 6–8

This is a traditional Syrian dip made from roasted sweet red peppers and walnuts.

Cook the peppers one at a time by skewering each one on a fork and holding it directly over a gas flame for 10–15 minutes, until the skin is blackened all over. Alternatively, put them on a baking sheet in an oven preheated to 220°C (425°F) Gas 7. Cook them for about 10–15 minutes, until the skin has puffed up and blackened all over. Transfer to a bowl, cover with clingfilm/plastic wrap and leave until cool enough to handle.

Using your hands, remove the skin and seeds from the peppers and tear the flesh into pieces. Put it in a food processor and add the remaining ingredients. Process to a coarse paste. Season to taste and transfer to a bowl. Cover with clingfilm/plastic wrap and refrigerate for 8 hours or ideally overnight before serving.

To serve, bring the dip to room temperature and transfer it to a shallow bowl. Drizzle with olive oil and sprinkle with chopped pistachios. Serve with toasted pitta or flatbread.

DUKKAH

20 g/1½ tablespoons blanched hazelnuts

20 g/1½ tablespoons blanched almonds

2 tablespoons sesame seeds

1 tablespoon cumin seeds

1 tablespoon coriander seeds

1 tablespoon dried mint

¼ teaspoon salt

extra virgin olive oil, to serve

chunks of crusty white bread, to serve

Serves 4

This dry Egyptian dip is eaten with bread dunked in olive oil so that the mix clings to it.

Preheat the oven to 180°C (350°F) Gas 4.

Roast the nuts on separate baking sheets; the hazelnuts for about 5 minutes and the almonds for about 8 minutes. Leave to cool. Meanwhile, in a dry frying pan/skillet set over a medium heat, fry the cumin seeds and coriander seeds for 1–2 minutes, until fragrant. In a food processor, blitz the spices, roasted nuts, seeds, dried mint and salt until finely ground. Be careful not too blend for too long, though, as the nuts will begin to release their oils and it will turn into a paste. Carefully spoon the mixture into a bowl. Serve with a dish of olive oil and chunks of bread for dipping.

WARM OLIVE & ARTICHOKE DIP

160 g/5½ oz. green pitted olives (drained weight), rinsed to remove excess brine

290 g/10 oz. chargrilled artichokes preserved in olive oil, drained

1 tablespoon Worcestershire sauce

1 teaspoon wholegrain mustard

150 ml/5 fl. oz. cup crème fraîche or sour cream

150 g/5½ oz. cream cheese

50 g/2 oz. Parmesan cheese, finely grated

freshly ground black pepper

warm crusty bread, to serve

Serves 6

This is a really savoury and moreish dip with a kick of saltiness from the olives and Parmesan. Use black olives in place of the green ones, if preferred.

Preheat the oven to 180°C (350°F) Gas 4.

Put the drained olives and artichokes in a food processor or blender and blitz until chopped into small pieces.

In a mixing bowl, whisk together the Worcestershire sauce, mustard, crème fraîche and cream cheese until smooth. Reserve a few tablespoons of the grated Parmesan and stir the rest into the mixture. Fold in the chopped artichokes and olives and mix well until everything is coated with the cream cheese mixture. Taste for seasoning – you shouldn't need to add any salt but add black pepper as required.

Spoon into an ovenproof dish and spread out in an even layer. Sprinkle the reserved Parmesan over the top and bake for 25–30 minutes until the Parmesan starts to turn golden brown on top. Remove from the oven and leave to cool slightly before serving.

Serve spread onto warm crusty bread.

BLACK OLIVE TAPENADE

1 garlic clove, crushed

freshly squeezed juice of 1 lemon

3 tablespoons capers, chopped

6 anchovy fillets, chopped

250 g/9 oz. black olives, pitted

leaves from a small bunch of fresh flat-leaf parsley, chopped

2–4 tablespoons extra virgin olive oil

salt and freshly ground black pepper

crusty bread and crudités, to serve

Serves 4

Here classic Mediterranean ingredients are combined to make simple yet flavoursome dip. Serve with crusty bread and crudités.

Tip the garlic, lemon juice, capers and anchovy fillets into a food processor and process for about 10 seconds.

Add the olives and parsley and just enough olive oil to make a paste. Season to taste if necessary. Scrape out into a small bowl and serve with crusty bread and crudités. The dip has a very strong flavour so a little goes a long way!

CHAPTER 5

YOGURT & CHEESE

RANCH DIP WITH SWEET POTATO CHIPS

Ranch dip is an all-American classic — perfect for serving at tailgate parties. It is light and refreshing and bursting with herb flavours.

60 ml/¼ cup buttermilk
150 g/5½ oz. cream cheese
40 ml/2½ tablespoons mayonnaise
1 garlic clove, peeled and chopped
1 tablespoon olive oil
freshly squeezed juice of ½ a lemon
1 tablespoon chopped fresh chives
1 tablespoon chopped fresh parsley
1 tablespoon chopped fresh dill
½ teaspoon paprika
1 teaspoon Dijon mustard
salt and freshly ground black pepper

FOR THE SWEET POTATO CHIPS
2 sweet potatoes
2 tablespoons sunflower oil
sprinkling of sea salt, to serve

Serves 6–8

In a bowl whisk together the buttermilk, cream cheese and mayonnaise until smooth.

Put the garlic, olive oil, lemon juice, chives, parsley and dill in a food processor and blitz until very finely chopped and the oil has emulsified. Make sure that there are no large pieces of garlic.

Fold the herb oil into the cream cheese mixture with the paprika and mustard, mixing well so that it is all combined. Season with salt and pepper.

Spoon into a serving bowl to serve.

For the chips, preheat the oven to 180°C (350°F) Gas 4. Using a mandolin or sharp knife, finely slice the sweet potato and pat dry. Toss the slices in sunflower oil and season with salt and pepper. Spread the veg on a lightly oiled baking sheet and bake for 10–15 minutes, then turn and bake for 5 minutes, or until crisp. Transfer to a wire rack to cool. Serve with a sprinkling of sea salt.

Variation Cheddar, bacon and onion ranch dip
Fry/sauté 4 rashers/slices of lean bacon until crisp and chop into small pieces. Allow to cool and stir into the dip (omitting the dill for the original recipe), along with 4 tablespoons grated/shredded cheddar cheese. Garnish with a handful of chopped spring onions/scallions and serve with giant pretzels for dipping.

ROAST GARLIC HERBED LABNEH

Making labneh (also labne, labni or yogurt cheese) is very simple, but do bear in mind that it takes 24 hours to strain the yogurt. Serve this Middle Eastern cheese with hot pitta bread or vegetable crudités.

450 g/2 cups full-fat goat's milk yogurt

salt

2 roast garlic cloves (page 23)

finely grated zest of 1 lemon

3 tablespoons finely chopped fresh flat-leaf parsley

1 teaspoon finely chopped fresh chives

1 teaspoon fresh thyme leaves

olive oil, to serve

pistachio nuts, finely ground, to garnish

hot pitta bread or vegetable crudités, to serve

a muslin/cheesecloth square and string

Serves 4–6

First make the labneh. Season the yogurt with salt to taste, mixing it in well. Put the yogurt in the centre of the muslin/cheesecloth square, fold up the muslin/cheesecloth around the yogurt and tie tightly, forming a parcel. Suspend the muslin/cheesecloth parcel over a deep, large bowl by tying it with string to a wooden spoon laid across the top of the bowl. Leave in the refrigerator for 24 hours, during which time the excess moisture will drip out of the parcel.

Squeeze the roast garlic out of the papery skin and mash into a paste. Flavour the labneh by mixing it with the roast garlic, lemon zest, parsley, chives and thyme.

Transfer the labneh to a dish. Use the back of a spoon to make a little hollow in the middle of the labneh, pour in a little olive oil, sprinkle with ground pistachio nuts and serve with hot pitta bread or vegetable crudités.

Variations

Labneh with dried and fresh mint Beat the labneh with 2–3 cloves crushed garlic and 1 tablespoon of dried mint. Fold in the leaves from a small bunch of fresh mint. Spoon into a bowl and drizzle with good olive oil.

Labneh with garlic, red chillies/chiles and dill Beat the labneh with 1 tablespoon of finely chopped red chilli/chile, 1 crushed garlic clove and 1 tablespoon of finely chopped fresh dill. Spoon into a bowl and garnish with a sprig of dill.

Labneh with harissa, coriander/cilantro and honey Beat the labneh with 2 crushed garlic cloves, ½ teaspoon salt, 2 teaspoons harissa paste, a handful of finely chopped fresh coriander/cilantro leaves and 1 tablespoon of runny honey. Spoon into a bowl and garnish with a sprig of coriander/cilantro.

ROASTED RED PEPPER RAITA

2 red (bell) peppers

1 teaspoon balsamic vinegar

1 teaspoon olive oil

a pinch of salt

400 g/14 oz. Greek/US strained plain yogurt

seeds of ½ a pomegranate

1 teaspoon sumac

spicy lentil chips or crackers, to serve

Serves 4–6

Serve this colourful, cooling dip as part of a summer appetizer. A spicy lentil chip or cracker work well as a dipper here.

Grill or roast the red peppers until they're charred on all sides. Wrap in a plastic bag (which makes them easier to peel afterwards), set aside to cool, then peel, deseed and chop into short strips.

Put the pepper strips in a bowl, add the balsamic vinegar, olive oil and salt and mix together.

Set a few of the pepper strips aside. Fold through the yogurt and stir in most of the pomegranate seeds, but set aside 1 tablespoon to garnish. Stir in ½ teaspoon sumac.

Just before serving, garnish the raita with the reserved pepper strips and pomegranate seeds, and sprinkle over the remaining sumac.

MARINATED FETA DIP

400 g/14 oz. feta cheese, cut into small chunks

400 ml/1¾ cups good-quality olive oil

grated zest of 1 lemon

1 tablespoon fennel seeds

1 red onion, thinly sliced

3 sprigs thyme or rosemary

Tortilla Chips (page 40) or chunks of bread, to serve

Serves 4

You'll need to make this at least a day ahead. You can pop whatever you like in the oil – from chillies/chiles to pink peppercorns. Make sure you serve tortilla chips or chunks of bread to spoon the cheese onto.

Put all the ingredients in a sterilized jar and pop it in the refrigerator for a few days. If you only have a night, warm the oil with everything except the cheese in a pan. Let it cool, then add the cheese and refrigerate, until you are ready to serve.

Serve with a spoon to remove the feta from the oil and tortilla chips or chunks of bread for dipping.

BLUE CHEESE & WALNUT DIP

100 g/3½ oz. walnut pieces or
halves

1 teaspoon finely chopped rosemary

½ teaspoon finely grated lemon zest

1 tablespoon olive oil

1 teaspoon caster sugar

salt and freshly ground black pepper

100 g/½ cup cream cheese

80 g/3 oz. Gorgonzola dolce or
other creamy blue cheese

60 ml/¼ cup sour cream

celery sticks, green apple wedges
or breadsticks

Serves 4–6

**If you prefer a really strong blue cheese
replace the Gorgonzola Dolce with stilton
or another hard blue cheese and blitz in a
blender with the sour cream until smooth
before adding to the dip.**

Preheat the oven to 180°C (350°F) Gas 4.

Put the walnuts, rosemary and lemon zest in a baking pan
and drizzle with the olive oil. Sprinkle over the sugar and
season with salt and pepper. Shake the pan so that all the
nuts are coated in the oil and herbs. Bake for about
5 minutes until the nuts are hot, taking care that they do
not burn. Remove from the oven and leave to cool.

Blitz three-quarters of the walnuts in a food processor or
blender. Tip the ground nuts into a bowl with the cream
cheese, blue cheese and sour cream and whisk together
until smooth and creamy with a slight nutty crunch. Season
to taste. Spoon the dip into a bowl and sprinkle over the
remaining roasted nuts.

Serve with celery sticks, apple wedges or breadsticks,
as preferred.

WHIPPED BLUE CHEESE DIP

150 g/scant ¾ cup Greek/US
strained plain yogurt

150 ml/scant ¾ cup sour cream

90 g/generous ¾ cup blue cheese,
such as Stilton or Gorgonzola

3 tablespoons mayonnaise

a pinch of salt

a splash of freshly squeezed lemon
juice

1 tablespoon chopped/snipped
chives, plus extra for decoration

carrot batons, to serve

Serves 4–6

**This recipe is for a lighter blue cheese dip
made with yogurt that is particularly delicious
served with crunchy carrot batons.**

Place all of the ingredients except the chives in a food
processor or blender, and blitz until smooth.

Transfer to a bowl and stir in the chopped/snipped chives.
Sprinkle some extra chives on top for decoration. Serve with
carrot batons.

PEA, FETA & FRESH MINT DIP

This dip is ideal for serving for a summer al fresco lunch. It is light and creamy with a perfect saltiness from the feta, and hints of lemon and mint make it really refreshing.

250g/9 oz. frozen peas

3 sprigs fresh mint

salt and freshly ground black pepper

zest and juice of 1 lemon

200g/7 oz. feta cheese

150g/5½ oz. cream cheese

peashoots, to garnish (optional)

olive oil, to serve

Pitta Chips (page 32) or Bagel Toasts (page 19), to serve

Serves 4

Bring a saucepan of water to the boil and simmer the peas with the mint and a pinch of salt for about 5 minutes until cooked. Drain and blanch in cold water until the peas are cold.

Drain the peas and add to a blender with the mint and the lemon juice. Blitz to a purée but keep some texture to it. If you prefer a very smooth dip you can pass the pea mixture through a fine mesh sieve/strainer using a rubber spatula or spoon.

Crumble the feta into a mixing bowl then whisk together with the cream cheese until smooth. Add the lemon zest, pea purée and a good grinding of black pepper and whisk again.

Spoon into a bowl and garnish with peashoots, if using, and a drizzle of olive oil. Serve with pitta chips or bagel toasts for dipping.

FRENCH ONION DIP WITH POTATO CHIPS

When onions are roasted, they develop a sweet and delicious caramel flavour, perfect for this tangy smoky dip which is something of a retro classic. Here it is served with deliciously light and crunchy homemade potato crisps/chips.

4 medium brown onions

5 sprigs fresh thyme

2 tablespoons olive oil

salt and freshly ground black pepper

250 g/9 oz. cream cheese, at room temperature

3 tablespoons crème fraîche

potato crisps/chip or crackers, to serve

FOR THE POTATO CRISPS/CHIPS

800 g/1¾ lb. small waxy fingerling potatoes, such as Anya, Pink Fir Apple or Kipfler

125 ml/½ cup olive oil

125 ml/½ cup vegetable oil

Serves 6

Preheat the oven to 180°C (350°F) Gas 4.

Peel the onions and cut them into quarters. Put the onions in a roasting pan, add the thyme sprigs and drizzle with the olive oil. Season well with salt and pepper and bake in the oven for 30–40 minutes until the onions are soft and have started to caramelize. Give them a stir towards the end of cooking so they don't burn. Remove from the oven and leave to cool. Discard any onions that have gone black as they will add a bitterness to the dip.

Remove the thyme sprigs and run your fingers along them to remove the leaves, reserving one sprig for garnish, if you wish. Add the leaves, and onions in their cooking juices, to a blender and blitz to a smooth purée.

Whisk the cream cheese into the crème fraîche and blend with the onion purée. Taste for seasoning, adding more salt and pepper if needed.

To make the potato chips, cut the potatoes into slices about 3 mm/⅛ in. thick. Bring a large saucepan of lightly salted water to the boil. Add the potatoes, cover the pan and remove from the heat. Leave in the hot water for 5 minutes. Drain well and arrange the slices on a wire rack in a single layer until completely cool.

Put the oils in a saucepan or large frying pan/skillet set over a high heat. When the oil is hot, cook the potato slices in batches for 5–6 minutes each, turning once or twice, until crisp and golden. Remove from the oil using a metal slotted spoon and drain on paper towels.

Spoon the dip into a bowl and garnish with the reserved thyme leaves. Serve with the warm potato chips, for dipping.

INDEX

FOOD PHOTOGRAPHY BY:

Peter Cassidy Page 47; Helen
Cathcart Pages 6, 26, 38;
Mowie Kay Pages 1–5, 9–21,
41–44, 48–53, 58–62; Lisa
Linder Endpapers; Steve Painter
Page 34; William Reavell Pages
25, 33; Clare Winfield Pages 22,
29, 30, 37, 54, 57.